Whatever life serves you, Cathy AJ Hardy has fashioned a small meditation to accompany you at this moment: Little word bouquets of feeling, of comfort, of praise, of gratitude, of sorrow, of love...

Find yours for the day and simply breathe with the small prayer and let it enter you where you are standing.

—Gertrud Mueller Nelson
Author of *To Dance with God*
and *Here All Dwell Free*.

 FriesenPress

One Printers Way
Altona, MB R0G 0B0
Canada

www.friesenpress.com

ISBN
978-1-03-915834-4 (Hardcover)
978-1-03-915833-7 (Paperback)
978-1-03-915835-1 (eBook)

1. POETRY, SUBJECTS & THEMES, INSPIRATION & RELIGIOUS

Distributed to the trade by The Ingram Book Company

LOVE

Breathes With Me

VOLUME II

A Book of Poems & Prayers

Cathy AJ Hardy

Table of Contents

Introduction

I have been inspired to write these simple prayers and poems from times of silence and solitude, from precious moments of sitting with another through spiritual companionship in the work I do as a spiritual director, from the longing to create new soul language for groups meeting together, and from a joy of expressing moments of my personal journey.

It is my hope and prayer that these words may open a pathway of soul connection for you – within your own life, with others, and with the Mystery of the Divine, however you understand this.

Although I come from a Christian mystical tradition in my day-to-day walk, I trust the language here will be broad enough to meet you where you are in your human story.

From the time I was a small child, there was a sense in me of the Mystery, a Beautiful Presence of Love, that has accompanied me throughout my life. I do not seek to explain this Presence, only to acknowledge that as I breathe, as I have life, as I participate in this human experience, my heart opens to a wonder of Life. This Mystery is at times as wide as the expanding universe and other times as intimate as breath.

Although I do not see clearly, hear fully, or understand completely, my soul says "yes" to this Beautiful Presence, and I trust that somehow these words of my heart will be a gift to you.

With love,
Cathy

Prayers

Alleluia

Source.
Breath in our breath.
Sound in our sound.
Light in our eyes.

Glistening of Spring.
Abundance of Summer.
Unravelling of Fall.
Depth of Winter.

Again and again,
the resurrection of Life,
the Song of all,
emerges
as
we partake, witness, celebrate
within us and outside of us
the wonder, glory, splendour, vibration,
the flow of blessing
that is Love,
that is
Alaha[1].
Home.
Being.
Vibrancy.
Unity of All.
Alleluia.

---

[1] Klotz, Neil Douglas, *Prayers of the Cosmos*, Alaha – Aramaic for 'God', literally meaning, "The Oneness" pg. 13 *Prayers of Cosmos*

Prayer of Fire
Inspired by the life of St. Brigid

Breathe on the embers within
for renewed hope, inspiration, and vision.

Breathe on the embers within
for renewed kindness, compassion, and mercy.

Breathe on the embers within
for renewed passion for justice, fierceness for generosity, and wildness
for love.

May this fire
be a light in shadowed times.

May this fire
be a solace of warmth; comfort for those who draw near.

May this fire
be a gathering place for souls to know sanctuary.

Keep the fire
burning beyond fatigue, discouragement, and fear.

Keep the fire
burning with intensity, creativity, and ingenuity.

Keep the fire
burning with desire, faithfulness, and steadfastness.

The sisters of St. Brigid kept the flame of fire burning in Kildare,
Ireland, for over 1000 years.

Prayer of Creation
Inspired by St. Patrick

I bind unto myself today the virtues of the star-lit heaven:
the ever-expanding creativity of the universe, spreading further and
further into the unknown, just as my soul continues to also expand and
move beyond known barriers; allowing the energy of Love to propel
the evolution of being within.

I bind unto myself today the glorious sun's life-giving rays:
the warmth and healing energy flowing into me and all of creation;
offering vitality, life, nurture and love into my body, heart and soul,
feeding the seeds of my heart so that they grow as an embryo within,
preparing for birth.

I bind unto myself today the whiteness of the moon at even:
the shimmer of light that shines in the deepest darkness, in times of
threshold between night and day, day and night, the tender light that
allows my heart to only see the next step, inviting me to trust in the
shadowlands of my life.

I bind unto myself today the flash of lightning free:
the radiance of awareness that sparks new understanding in the
season of storm and upheaval, the wildness of light that allows the
whole sky to radiate with beauty amidst the rumble and tumble of
the unknown.

I bind unto myself today the wildness of wind:
the force of Love that shakes loose the leaves of my tree that need to fall, allowing the exposing beauty of the new buds to be seen underneath where I saw only emptiness. The sweeping energy that brings a holy disruption into spaces that have become old and stagnant. The tender gentle winds that offer hope on a spring morning.

I bind unto myself today the stable earth:
the rock beneath my feet I can rest on, the foundation of Love I can allow my heart to root in and find solace, the depths of soul within that is eternal.

I bind unto myself today the deep salt sea:
the wide and expansive waters reminding us of the Womb of Love from which we all came, the oceanic darkness of formation which brought us into life, the mystery of depths that is ineffable.

I bind unto myself today the fullness of Love,
the grace of Mercy,
the beauty of Wisdom.

Words in italics are from the prayer "Deer's Cry", attributed to St. Patrick.

Prayer of Binding to Love

I bind my mind to the infinite Love of the universe;
to know the truth of my name, my being, my value, my belonging,
and my home.
I bind my thoughts to be attentive to the wonder and truth of Love,
to be attuned to the inspiration and creativity of the Divine.
I bind my mind to Love.

I bind my heart, my passion, to the Infinite Flow of Life;
tapping into the wellspring of veriditas[2], creativity, truth, grace, and beauty,
this inner reality where the Infinite is infinite in possibility.
I bind my heart to Love.

I bind my eyes to see the way Love sees;
to see from the soul within, from a place of compassion,
truth, and insight.
I bind my eyes to Love.

I bind my ears to sounds Love is inviting me to hear;
the silent whispers, songs, invitations and callings that
emerge in both darkness and light.
I bind my ears to Love.

---

2   Veriditas is a word from the mystic Hildegarde of Bingen, and means 'mighty
     green-ness', a term she used for the energizing presence of God.

I bind my mouth to speak truth; to be in union with the way of Love,
through word and through silence, through song and melody,
through what is spoken and unspoken,
realizing the power and aliveness that comes through our lips.
I bind my mouth to Love.

I bind my feet to the path of purpose, of union with Love,
of flow with Mystery, of partnership with Life,
of vitality that emerges when my life, my vocation,
my life's movement is in alignment with my soul.
I bind my feet to Love.

I bind these hands to receive from the Infinite
the inheritance I am invited to embrace;
gifts that remind me of the truth of my soul,
the belonging to the Beloved and the tools for service.

I bind these hands to bless;
to create, to write, to touch, to love, to serve,
to move out of the overflow of the abundance of the well-spring.
I bind my hands to Love.

I bind my whole life to Love;
to the way of Love,
the truth of Love, the generosity of Love, the partnership of Love.
I am my Beloved's and the Beloved is mine.
The banner of my life is Love.
The banner over life is Love.

Prayers for Gatherings

Prayers for Healing

For the aspects of our lives that feel shattered, torn, fractured,
and distressed.
Mercy.
For the aspects of our lives that are sick, diseased, malnourished, and frail.
Mercy.

For elements of our communities that are in disrepair, break-down,
and pain.
Mercy
For elements of our communities that are suffering, wounded, and hurting.
Mercy.

For Mother Earth who is undergoing climate crisis and upheaval.
Mercy.
For brother and sister creatures who are impacted by the
changing environment.
Mercy.

May we receive healing in our bodies.
May we receive healing in our spirits.
May we receive healing in our relationships.
May we receive healing in our communities.

May our Earth Mother receive healing.
May all of creation receive healing.

May healing ignite a resurrection of possibility
in body, soul, and mind;
for each one of us,
**for our communities
and for our planet.**

We Open

One: O Great Friend, we open our hearts

One: We open ...   All: **to awareness of Presence**

We open ...   **to receive Divine grace**

We open ...   **for the restoration of our souls**

We open ...   **for healing of the body**

We open ...   **for mercy in our brokenness**

We open ...   **for forgiveness of where we have erred**

We open ...   **for guidance on the way**

We open ...   **for truth in our hearts**

We open ...   **for the baptism of Love**

We Look to You

One: Creator, Redeemer & Healer
    All: We look to You
One: Luminous Light
    All: We look to You
One: Radiant Love
    All: You look to us
One: Source of All
    All: You look to us
One: Ancient of Days
    All: Living within
One: Compassionate Friend
    All: Living within
One: Love Eternal
    All: Radiant and overflowing
        Generative and creative
        Living within
        Flowing through
        Breathing, Creating, Living ... in us
        Living ... through us.
One: Thank you
    All: Thank you
        Thank you

We Return

O Eternal Presence,
    We return through silence.
O Eternal Love,
    We return through stillness.
O Eternal Birther,
    We return through listening.
O Eternal Friend,
    We return though breathing.

You have set the table.
    We come and receive.
You welcome us with joy.
    We dare to open our hearts.
You sing over us with love.
    We sing our response in gratitude.

    May what is eternal in us flow with the Eternal.
    May what is love in us flow with the Great Love.

Align Us

Awaken us, align us.
Restore us, remember us.
May we return once again
And live from the reflection of Love.

Fear has gripped us.
Doubt has paralyzed us.
We have lost sight of hope.
We have lost sight of one another.

We open our hearts.
Awaken us, align us once again.
May we return to the Source of Lives.
And live from the reflection of Joy.

Align us to the yearnings of creation.
Align us to the breath of the earth.
Align us to the expansiveness of the galaxies.
Align us to the depths of the sea.

Align us to the silence of the stars.
Align us to the song of the birds.
Align us with the wildness of the ocean.
Align us with the stillness of the night.

Advent Prayer

O Radiance of Light,
> **We are recalled to the story of humble beginnings.**

O Radiance of Darkness,
> **We are recalled to the story of the unexpected.**

O Radiance of Mystery,
> **We are recalled to the story of new life.**

O Radiance of Song,
> **We are recalled to the mystery of Love with us.**

As we rest in the deepest darkness of the year,
> **We awaken to the light rising.**

As we wait in the deepest darkness of the year,
> **We awaken to the gifts of longing in the unknown.**

As we hope in the deepest darkness of the year,
> **We listen for the song of the Eternal.**

As we sing in the deepest darkness of the year,
> **We open to the harmony of the spheres.**

> **May we be recalled to the truth and beauty of our souls.**
> **May we be recalled to the wonder of this season.**

Kyrie, Kyrie, Eleison

For those suffering around the world; in sickness, in danger, in war, in inner turmoil, we pray...

For those in positions of power; for integrity, kindness, wisdom, insight and courage, we pray...

For those in division; for the ability to listen, to pause, to be open, to be gentle, we pray...

For those in service to others; for sustenance, provision, encouragement and grace, we pray...

For our children and our children's children; for imagination, for hope, for playfulness, for new ideas, for creativity, for vitality of life, we pray...

For our own lives; for the ability to listen, to have mercy, to know compassion, to live in integrity of soul, to be faithful, we pray...

Speak out a Name for Prayer...

In You Our Souls Wait in Silence

Meditation inspired from Psalm 63 & Isaiah 30:15

All: In You our souls wait in silence
> O Living Presence, our Source.
> We pause with heart, mind and strength.
> We pause, listen and open our awareness.
> We rest and wait, listening in the quiet.

All: In You our souls wait in silence
> Our souls thirst for comfort and peace.
> We yearn to be renewed
> in a dry and tired land where there is no water.
> We come, we pause, we open, we listen.

All: In You our souls wait in silence
> At night our hearts turn to meditate in the stillness.
> We ponder through the hours of darkness.
> For Love has been our help.
> Love has been our sustenance and strength.

All: *In You our souls wait in silence*

In quietness and trust we are renewed and find strength.
And we sing for joy in the shelter of Love's wings.
For we have tasted beauty and mystery, even in times of shadow.
We have seen reflections of Love in moments of grace.

All: *In You our souls wait in silence*

Our souls hold fast to the kindness of Love.
Love's tender mercy holds us up.
We find our peace when we pause and wait.
We will abide in Love, with hearts of gratitude.

All: *In You our souls wait in silence*

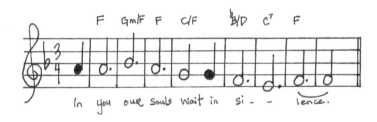

Blessings

Blessing of Creation

The untamed fragrance of the earth rises to meet me.
I receive.
The deep stability of the mountains settles me.
I receive.
The constant beauty of evergreens comforts me.
I receive.
The steady flow of the river washes me.
I receive.
The gentle radiance of the moon whispers to me.
I receive.
The nourishing warmth of the sun kisses me.
I receive.
The fresh unfolding of ferns awakens hope in me.
I receive.
The silent soaring of the eagle revives me.
I receive.
The call of the hidden owl stirs the heart of me.
I receive.

All creation pulsates with aliveness, with beauty, with glory;
speaking, shining, blessing, embracing.
I receive.

May my eyes see the blessing.
May my ears hear the blessing.
May my heart open to receive the blessing.
May my life carry the blessing of creation within.

In the Midst

May you know grace
in your times of longing without knowing.
May you know grace
in your prayers of groaning with sorrow.
May you know grace
in your nights of sighing and tears.
May you know grace
in your passage of disorientation and confusion.
May you know grace
as you stand on thresholds you have never known before.
May you know grace
in seasons of dying and releasing what now is ready for passage.
May you know grace
to be courageous in deepest night when dawn has not yet come.
May you know grace
to sing again when the morning light rises.
May you know grace
in receiving mercy in the midst of it all.

Face to Face

May you know the gentle hands of Love on your forehead.
May you know the sweet breath of Love on your face.
May you know the upholding strength of Love at your back.
May you know the undergirding support of Love under your feet.
May you know the well of Love's creativity rising from your belly.
May you know the wideness of Love's mercy in your heart.
May you know the kindness of Love in your eyes.
May you know the song of Love in your ears.
May you know the call of Love in your soul.
May you lose track of where you end and Love begins.
May you dance all your days in the flow of union with this Love
until you meet
face to face.

A Blessing for Difficult Days

May we know the grace of stillness
in the intensity of chaos.

May we know the grace of wisdom
in the face of decision making.

May we know the grace of equanimity
in the midst of anxiety.

May we know the grace of kindness
in the midst of fear.

May we know the grace of patience
in the midst of stress.

As Love has guided all generations in times of turmoil,
may Love guide us now.

As Love has whispered to individuals and communities in times
of challenge,
may we listen now.

As Love has guided individuals to lead and to guide in times
of desperation,
may wise leaders rise up now.

As Love has guided individuals to pray, to serve, to love,
may many follow the call to prayer, to serve, to love now.

May our intentions, our decisions, our actions,
be rooted and grounded in Love.
May all we are, say and do flow out of communion of Friendship with
the Beloved.

Love giving strength.
Love giving guidance.
Love giving courage.
Love giving insight.
Love giving wisdom.

May we live the blessing of the Love we have known.

Poetry & Ponderings

Still Point at the Centre

The still point anchors our souls,
rooting us in a constant embrace.
It is the place where we are recalled, returned, and remembered
to the inseparable Love of the Divine.
All movement flowing from the inner sanctum,
the inner sanctuary of the soul,
is rooted in this Love.
This Love is the silent point of nothing and everything.
All is found in the one centre.
This inner sanctuary is a place of profound stillness, silence and possibility.
It is the ground of all being, the birthplace of Life.
We are invited to root ourselves in this centre,
where we return to our original consciousness,
the original essence out of which we came;
the dwelling place of Love.
Love is at the centre of our being.

The journey, in a down ... to the stillpoint within ... home of your soul ... Love it, the centre of your being, You are invited to enter...

O Great Pine

Your trunk is large
and emanates
a beautiful strength
I receive
in the cells of my soul
when I am near you.

You are still
yet somehow ...
vibrant ... alive ... bubbling ...
with a quiet energy.

I look way up
and can't see the heights of you.
I look down
and know
you live also in mystery -
with dark, hidden places
I am unable to touch.

When the storm comes
you bend ...
and with gentle dignity, remain.
When the skies open with light,
your green nettles
glisten with living
possibility.

You deepen into the earth
with your silent
rootedness.
You expand into sky,
exploring your
fullness of being.

O Great Pine,
be my teacher.
O Great Pine,
be my teacher.

Listening

Here I am.
Tempted by distraction.
Lured by possibilities
that pull me away
from being
present,
attentive.
However, I come.
Here
I
Am.
Allowing my body
to return
to this moment.
This moment
that requires a relinquishment;
a relinquishment
of control.
This moment
that invites ...
an emptiness of being.

An emptiness that opens
my heart,
my soul,
into an inner posture
of receptivity, of
listening.
Listening invites
a nakedness, a vulnerability
a space,
a space
within,
where the heart
can receive
a touch;
a touch of the mystery
of grace.
Here I am.
I am
Listening.

Belonging

It can feel like nothing
This place
That is
Everything
It is the space beyond
The breath in
The void
If one allows
Oneself to stay
And not escape
The emptiness
The open vastness
Of unknowing
The stark reality of nothingness
In the present
Moment
A taste of wonder
Arises
Like the first

Rays of dawn
On a winter
Morning
A moment
Of expanse
Space
Between
Inhale and exhale
Where one remembers
Home
Union with Love
Belonging
Forever
In the heart
Of the Universe

Could it be?

Could it be
that our strength will come
from entering
a stillness of heart?

Could it be
we will know renewal of heart
by allowing
a slower pace of being?

Could it be
that we will know courage
by trusting
beyond our knowing?

Could it be
that we will taste joy
from surrender
into Love?

Intimate as Breath

Beyond
understanding
grasp
language
image
projection

Beyond
theology
institution
names
control
boxes
comfort

A taste
A glimpse
A moment
A shiver

Awakens ...
breathes us
back
into knowing
we are part
of
a whole
that is
beyond
all concepts
and yet,
within ...
intimate
as
breath

Silence is My Medicine

Silence is my medicine.
I used to be afraid of the silence,
filling it with fearful comments,
afraid to be seen in my fragility,
afraid to be known in my inadequacy.

To allow silence
forced me to face my pain, my panic,
my sense of unworthiness,
and tumble in and down
to what I perceived as the dark,
shadowy and horrid aspects of self.

It was a terror
to go in and down.
What would I see?
What would I face?

A clear diamond awaited me,
glistening radiance in all directions,
slowly turning in ravishing beauty.
"This is who you are," the Great Silence spoke.

"In and down ...
in your depth and darkness
is a treasure,
your greatest treasure,
your soul."

The Great Silence enfolded me
like a mother with child.
A warm and spacious, kind and tender Silence,
who became my teacher, my friend,
my guide, my medicine.

The Great Silence healed my mind
of the toxic chemicals born from self-loathing.
The Great Silence healed my heart
of the raging pain from self-rejection.

The Great Silence led me to treasure
the treasure of soul.
And together,
we made a garden
in the deep, dark soil of my being.

We planted ferns, moss and maple trees.
We built bridges, pathways and sacred places
For others to come and sit awhile.

We restored ancient vines that had come over the old century walls,
pruning and taking away dead branches from times past ...
until they gleamed and glistened again with life.

We wrote songs
from the spacious beauty of the garden,
filling the air with golden beams of sunlight.
And the birds came,
joining us in the chorus.

Together,
the Great Silence and I
made a home,
the home I had always
been searching for,
not knowing
this home
is my very life.

Transcendence

My face re-enters the dirt,
the fleshy earth of forest.
Face down into darkness,
I yield to the quiet
and plunge my soul yet again
into formation,
another chrysalis of unknown.
I yield my body
and sink
into the smells of soil;
pine needles, moss and worms.
I let go
of sky and expanse
and rest
in this posture
of falling
into Mother.
It is time for another gestation.
And so, back into her womb I go.
Fall, fall, fall.

Loosening my grip on
what has become familiar,
what has brought security... safety ...
and
let
go.

Disorientation welcomes me:
"Come, darling.
Come once again into Mother.
Release your grip and
tumble back in."

The familiar warmth
of darkness tucks me in,
back into the folds
of unknowing,
that familiar place of surrender
to Love,

the space of waiting
and allowing,
where emptiness turns into
spaciousness.

Love takes my body,
dissolved yet again
into caterpillar soup
and weaves a wonder
of alchemy,
a dance of Love
expressed
in the cells of my being.

A knowing
rises again in my soul
that life emerges from death,
for
transcendence
shines
from the darkness
of the womb.

Communion

What does one do,
when the heart leaks open
with aching love?
I look at the open sky and tears spill over.
"I love you."
"I love you," I cry out.
I turn to Cedar, rising majestically
before me. She shares
her fanned-out, glistening-with-green
branches for me to carry her scent
into my dwelling place.
"Thank you, my friend Cedar.
I love your silent ways, your ever-vibrant faithfulness."
I hold Lemon for my tea,
slicing her open, noticing the plump juiciness of her being.
"I love you, Lemon, so radiant in your golden glory.
You open and create a nutritious drink for me.
You are filled with abundance,
carrying seeds for generations to follow.
Thank you, thank you."
I gaze towards Mountain, who has
companioned me
since my earliest memories.
"Thank you, thank you.

I love you too. I love your beauty.
You are solid, stable,
a point of reference in the geography of my life.
You invite me to look up and to see
beyond the valley.
I love you. I love you."
Salty fluid is flowing in a gentle stream down my cheek.
Why do I feel so deeply? – I don't know – but I do.
I feel the connection,
the communion of these earthy saints,
and love in return.
I feel Mountain gazing at me,
calling out to remember rest and quiet
in the midst of storm.
I see Lemon smiling at me,
reminding me of freshness, abundance
and new life when I pay attention.
I feel the gentle kindness of Cedar,
caressing my hands and hugging my life,
providing shelter of beauty in times of war.
"We love you. We love you." I hear them say.
They are my dear friends,
companions in the day to day of life.

We see each other
and share
a communion of silence,
of grace,
of love.
My friends know how to heal me
when my human friends
are not close by or
don't know what to say.
These silent friends shelter me
and tell me they understand, they know.
They heal me where I am tired,
where I am worn thin
by the
suffering of the world,
where my nerves are frayed
and my mental state is
fragile from tending souls.
These ones gather me up,
wrapping me in
a blanket of cloud and sunbeams,
singing to my heart,
restoring, reviving,
renewing me.
Communion of Saints.
Communion of Souls.
"Oh, how I love you.
Oh, how I love you.
Thank you."

Turning

Turning.
Love is turning
my sadness
into
radiance.

Oh Beloved,
turn this sadness into radiance
as I merge the heart of me,
the body of me,
the energy of me,
the reality of me
into the Heart of Love,
which is deeper
than the great ocean of sadness
in which I swam for so many years.

May the tide of Love
sweep me further
into underground living waters,
where the Sound of Laughter
is heard from my very bones,
where the song of joy
erupts like fire from my lips
and radiance
shines
from my soul.

I Choose You

I choose you,
dear heart.
I hold you
with tenderness
I cherish you.
I turn towards
the truth that you carry.
I envelop
the wounds that you bear.
I treasure you,
dear heart
You are my greatest possession.
You are beautiful beyond measure.

Within

It is dark
in the womb of God
It is a place of *sensing* and *awareness*
more than concrete facts
My body becomes aware of a Reality
that I am
within
I am **within** a Great Heart of Love
There is nowhere to 'go'
Nothing to 'do'
Because I am within
The Womb of God
is my sanctuary
Sacred, holy, beyond language
If I am still
I become aware
of the Heartbeat of Love
Resounding, resounding
I float and close my eyes
I rest
I rest
deeply
here

Knowing, really knowing,
that I am
within
and there is nothing
that will change that
Even though it is dark
it is a *warm* darkness
Like the place of moist earth
Where things grow and are nurtured
When I am still
I become aware
Of Love humming
And singing over me
What are the words I hear so faintly?
What is the melody of this song?
All I know is that it is tender
It is kind
It is sweet
It is safe
It is ***home***

Friend to My Own Dear Heart

When I edit my inner voice,
I silence my fullness of being.
When I am overwhelmed
with emotion or circumstance,
I am tempted to shut down
aspects of self
for protection and safety.
However, healing leads us to integrate
all the parts of us,
to become safe with ourselves.
The invitation is to turn towards.
Always.
We are invited to
turn towards
that which needs attention,
care, tenderness … kindness.
I am invited to learn how
to be a friend
to my own dear heart.
By turning towards,
Turning towards.

Wrestling

I am like Jacob
Wrestling with the angel.
I'm angry, confused, unsure.
I'm tired, fed up, impatient.
I'm annoyed, scared, furious.

How dare you guide me here?
I kick and punch and attack.
We wrestle to the ground and I release my venom.
Wrestling.
Fighting.

I'm fighting with the Eternal.
I don't understand.
I punch.
I kick.
I'm wrestling.
Angry woman that I am.

Pause.

Prayer.
Whatever that is.

Something shifts in my soul
in the hours of darkness.
In the hours of struggle.
In the hours of honest anguish.

After wrestling, wrestling, wrestling,
I kneel.
I surrender my life once again
into what I do not know,
what is beyond
my understanding;
the Mystery of Love,
the Mystery of Presence,
the Mystery of the Universe.

I allow.
I trust, or perhaps,
just dare to try
to trust
... even in unknowing.

Silence.
Tears.
Night falls.

Day breaks.

Awareness emerges with the rays of daylight.
– I am made from the laughter of God.
I am created from the essence
of the laughter of the Universe.
I am laughter.
I am the essence of God.

And in the awareness,
a song tumbles across the tundra ...
riveting my soul,
"Those that wrestle with God are friends of God.
You ... are friend of God."

Tears.
Tears.
Tears.
Those who wrestle are friends.
I am friend of the Universe.

May my life smell like roses.
May I leave the scent of roses behind me.

The Wise Crone

She is safe for my confidences
She isn't overwhelmed by me
She can hold her ground and not be hooked emotionally by me
She helps me find my inner wisdom and know my own ground
She doesn't make my story about 'her' story
She is emotionally stable and clear
She doesn't pity me
She doesn't rescue me
Ultimately, she trusts I will 'know'
I can be fragile as well as fierce in her presence
She cheers for me as I fly
And comforts me when I am hurting
I can feel her wildness
Exuding from her pores
I can sense deep wisdom in her eyes
I feel safe in the embrace of her arms
I am aware of her fierceness for my life
I see her scars and know she knows the path
& I trust her.

Jesu

Jesu.
Yeshua.
My friend.
My teacher
and guide
into the heart
of Love.
Your posture
of grace
continues
to transform
my being.
Grace.
And more grace.
Kindness
and wild courage.
You breathe
With me
And invite me
To know
The song
Of the Eternal.

Pilgrimage

Travelling solo ...
A rather naked journey.
Exposed
to the rawness of one's vulnerability
and the beauty of one's courage.

There is something one has to discover within –
to make decisions, to step out,
to read a map, to buy a ticket, to get on a train,
to walk alone in a city
where one has not been before.

If one can allow the unfolding of the path,
day by day,
there are surprises
that come towards the traveller;
as if the world was waiting for you
to step in and take a look around,
and be welcomed.

These moments
are not in the itinerary,
they are gifts; graces to receive:
An unexpected conversation with a stranger, now friend.
An unexpected turn of the road that leads to the perfect spot.
The dance of a bird that seems to be just for you.

And so, one realizes
that we are each part
of this beautiful world
and that this earth
is home for us all.

Emergence

Becoming.
Becoming.
One doesn't know what one is
when emerging from the cocoon.
One has surrendered in darkness and let go.
Period.
One does not attain emergence ...
– it unfolds unexpectedly,
like a fern in April;
a blob of dark matter evocatively rising
from the depth of earth
after a long, bitter winter.
Shocking green tentacles slowly,
yet unabashedly,
unfold outwards
towards glittering sunlight,
expanding with radiant surges of joy
in a wild display of beauty
filling empty space
with an eternal song
that echoes out to the stars.

Bow & Arrow

The pulling back of the bow
is an energetic reality in my life.

Surrender to the hands
that have formed me and hold me,
is the constant invitation.

My life is the bow,
stretching me way, way back
– into depths of silence and solitude;
that I may fly clear, straight, direct,
in the response of my life.

From the dream
at the hearth of my heart
to the horizon beyond my own imagination,
I've been taken to lands
beyond my knowing,
discovering possibilities
only Love could have foreseen
when thrusting me out
beyond the silence
to the shores of becoming.

Silence

Silence is our teacher.
Silence is our medicine.
Silence is our theology.

Silence evokes truth under chaos.
Silence evokes clarity in a storm.
Silence evokes the power of wisdom in times of anxiety.

Silence illuminates understanding.
Silence illuminates a possibility.
Silence illuminates the path of courage.

Silence holds presence.
Silence releases presence.
Silence births presence.

Silence opens the way of compassion.
Silence opens the way of kindness.
Silence opens the way of humility.

Fog

I do not know where I am going.
The fog kisses my hand
as I reach to feel my way forward.
The blindfold is firmly
in place and my eyes have surrendered
once again to the obscurity of darkness.

So many questions.
So much I do not understand.
I do not have answers,
only the path before me.

Gently, tenderly,
one small step at a time,
I walk.
Yearning only to stay in the flow,
yearning only to
follow the scent
of Love.

And In It All

To live with soul
   is to embrace all of life.
      To look, really look – and not turn away.
         To not turn away … from sadness, anger,
            mess, confusion,
               dissonance, despair, sorrow.

To not turn away … from joy,
   creativity, exuberance,
      laughter, excess, playfulness,
      sensuality, wildness.

      To live with soul
         is to be
            in each moment
               fully, to be present to
                  what is, to know.

To live with soul is not to cling …
   to another, to an experience, to a feeling …
      but rather to engage with the whole self;
         heart, mind, body.

We learn life here.
We learn love here.
We learn holiness here, the preciousness of life.

It is not all to be understood
    or fixed
        or attained
           or mastered.

           Rather,
           it is simply
           to be lived.

           And in it all ...
              to love.

CPSIA information can be obtained
at www.ICGtesting.com
Printed in the USA
BVHW042007061222
653581BV00001B/4